Boboli
Gardens

LITTA MEDRI
Director of the Boboli Gardens

GIORGIO GALLETTI
Director of Villas, Parks, and Gardens' Office

sillabe

ISBN 88-86392-57-5
© 1998 s i l l a b e s.r.l.
piazza Damiano Chiesa, 49 - 57124 Livorno
tel. 0586.867034 - fax 0586.869119

managing editor: Maddalena Paola Winspeare
graphic design and cover: Laura Belforte
editing: Federica Lehmann
translation: Anthony Cafazzo

lay-out: Franco Bulletti
photolithography: La Nuova Lito-Firenze

reproduction rights:
Archivio sillabe
Archivio Fotografico della Soprintendenza
per i Beni Ambientali e Architettonici
di Firenze, Pistoia e Prato

Contents

The garden complex of Boboli, which is covered exhaustively in this convenient guidebook, constitutes one of the most exquisite, perhaps grandest, example of those designs which have contributed to forging in the collective consciousness the image of the consummate garden alla italiana. Despite the extensive tampering it has suffered over the course of its long history (in particular, the 1834 destruction of the labyrinths to make way for the carriageable path) and the changes due to the natural life-cycle and replacement of its plant-life, Boboli still maintains in a clearly recognisable form the architectural and decorative setting conceived of in the early 16th C by its creator, 'Il Tribolo', that is, the characteristic formal Italian garden.

Accordingly, the garden's most distinguishing features are its plentiful flowing waters and monumental fountains, rich variety of grottoes, and multitude of marble sculptures and decorative elements arranged along its walks to focus the spectacular visual perspectives and highlight the rhythmic cadence of its plant-life. The countless modifications performed over the centuries have fitted in well with the strict criteria of 16th C design, reaching their culmination in the judicious addition of the large 18th C Lemon House, the functional Kaffeehaus and graceful new monumental gate in Via Romana, known as the 'Annalena Gate'. Thus, taken together, the gardens, monuments and statues of Boboli constitute a true open-air museum, a designation which recently has finally been granted after the long struggle of the Municipal Administration against those who would reduce Boboli to the more modest rank of 'local garden'.

The complete fencing in of the entire complex grounds and the institution of round-the-clock security and an entrance fee have restored due attention to a garden that rightfully belongs amongst Florence's most distinguished museum facilities.

It is however a museum needy of constant care and maintenance of all its holdings: the architectural structures and monuments, the decorative plants and outstanding botanical collections, such as the citrus and aquatic plants, are all threatened equally by natural ageing, the deteriorating effects of the elements and, at times, mankind's negligence. Programmatic, repeated cycles of maintenance, and the more incisive restorative works constantly occupy gardeners, art historians and architects in the effort to preserve and maintain the Boboli Gardens for the pleasure and enlightenment of an ever-growing public, and thus enable us to pass on to future generations this extremely fragile treasure, upheld as it is by a very delicate balance. It is a treasure which, in the sum total of its myriad historical, artistic, scientific and botanical composition, represents the summit of knowledge - the external manifestation of the highest role of culture and power. Small wonder that some of the most illustrious figures of European history coveted it so avidly, or that they went to such lengths, in energy and expense, to foster its continued development.

Mario Augusto Lolli Ghetti
Superintendent of Arts and Culture
for Florence, Pistoia and Prato

THE 16TH CENTURY

Agnolo Bronzino (Florence 1503-72), Portrait of Eleonora of Toledo with her son, Giovanni, *oil on canvas, 115 × 96 cm, Florence, Galleria degli Uffizi.*

The present-day Boboli Garden complex is the result of the union of the hill-side garden beyond the villa that Eleonora of Toledo, wife of Duke Cosimo I de' Medici, acquired in 1550 from the Pitti family, and the great expanse of land, originally given over to agriculture, bordered by the ramparts that the selfsame Cosimo I built during the war against Siena (1546-48) and the 14th C wall, its Roman Gate and the houses in via Romana. Already in the Late Middle Ages the area was known as "Boboli", a toponym used at the time to indicated wooded areas. The initial project envisaged the transforma-

tion of the *Orto de' Pitti* ('Pitti Orchard') into a garden setting worthy of the regal palace that Cosimo planned to realise there.

The original project was by Niccolò Pericoli, known as 'Il Tribolo' (Florence 1500-50), the Duke's favoured artist and creator of the Medici gardens in Villa in Castello. Upon the death of Il Tribolo, supervision of the work passed on to Davide Fortini, who was in turn succeeded by Giorgio Vasari from 1554 to 1661 and, finally by Bartolomeo Ammannati (ca 1560-83). With the advent of Francesco I (1574), the artist Bernardo Buon-

Agnolo Bronzino (Florence 1503-72), Cosimo I de' Medici in armour, *tempera on wood panel, 74 × 58 cm, Florence, Galleria degli Uffizi.*

talenti rose to eminence, and it was he who completed the Grand Grotto (also called Buontalenti's Grotto, 1583-93).

Despite the succession of overseers, Il Tribolo's original design was followed closely: as in the Gardens of Castello, the hill and valley behind the palace were subdivided into a grid of perpendicular compartments, filled with either abundant grape-vines and olive trees, or copses crossed by high espaliers, according to a typically Tuscan layout, termed *ragnaie*, that is, copses crisscrossed by frameworks hung with bird-hunting nets called *ragne*.

The stone quarry at the foot of Belvedere Hill was transformed into a semi-eliptical open space which followed the design of Roman hippodromes, though copses of various tree species were planted in place of the usual tiered stands. The area was called the Amphitheatre, and later, the wings of the palace courtyard (1561) would be designed by Bartolomeo Ammannati to fit this structure's U shape. Thus, the Pitti Palace and Boboli Gardens were to become a single indivisible architectural unit.

The Ocean Fountain, first documented in 1577 as standing in the Amphitheatre's arena, was sculpted by Giam-

bologna on a huge granite slab brought from Elba Island by order of Cosimo I de' Medici, moulded by Il Tribolo and later moved to the centre of the Island. The Grotto of Madam, work of Davide Fortini and Marco del Tasso (1553-55) dates back to the gardens' origins. A dwarf fruit-tree grove, considered particularly precious by Cosimo I, was planted nearby.

The Grand Grotto was begun under Vasari's supervision (1557) and brought to completion by Ammannati and Buontalenti between 1583 and 1593. The first stage in the gardens' history ended under Ferdinando I (Grand Duke, 1587 to 1609).

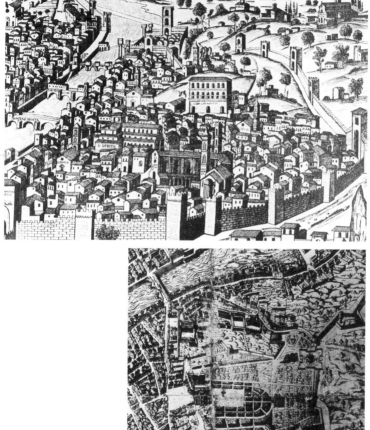

View of the Amphitheatre and Pitti Palace.

Perspective map, known as 'the chain', 1470, Florence, Museo "Firenze com'era".

Stefano Buonsignori, Map of Florence in 1584, Florence, Museo "Firenze com'era".

THE 17TH CENTURY

Romolo Ferrucci del Tadda, Fountain of the Mostaccini, pietra forte, 1619-21, detail.

Under Cosimo II (Grand Duke from 1609 to 1621) the gardens were expanded beyond the walls erected during the war against Siena. The work of extending the grounds, of which we have documents dating back to 1612, was overseen by Gherardo Mechini and Giulio Parigi. The garden's axis became the wide Cypress Lane that leads to the striking Island Pond, begun in 1612 and completed sometime before 1620. South of the lane, three large labyrinths were planted (eventually destroyed in 1834), as well as a walkway covered by holm-oak branches (the *Cerchiata grande* or 'Large Latticework') which is crossed midway by Cypress Lane and yet two more long, covered passages parallel to it (*Cerchiate piccole* or 'Small Latticework').

The *ragnaie* surrounding the Amphitheatre once provided a spectacular sequence of perspectives: first, the large *Ragnaia* of the Island, which hid the Island Pond from view, creating a surprise effect, and then the *Ragnaia della Pace* ('of Peace') under the 14th century walls, animated by bird troughs and a very long water 'chain', still in existence today and known as the Fountain of the Mostaccini. The spectacular culmination of the garden was the Island Pond, also designed by Giulio Parigi, which was begun in 1612 and described for the first time in 1620 by the poet Raffaello Chiabrera.

The Island was originally conceived of as a garden for the cultivation of citrus fruit and flowers. In all probability, a Venus fountain once stood in its centre but was removed by order of Grand Duke Ferdinando II in 1636 and substituted with Giambologna's Ocean Fountain.

It was Cosimo II who also had the idea of transforming the Amphitheatre into a masonry structure, though the actual work of this modification was begun only in 1630 under Grand Duke Ferdinando II, according to a project attributed rather uncertainly to Giulio Parigi and completed in 1636 under the guidance of Alfonso Parigi il Giovane. The current location of the statue of *Plenty* (begun by Giambologna and completed by Pietro Tacca) dates back to 1636 and represents the idealised end point of the line of sight which runs from Pitti Palace along the length of the axis formed by the Amphitheatre and Forcone Basin.

Stefano della Bella, Scenes from Atlantis from the ballet on horseback Il mondo festeggiante, *performed in the Amphitheatre in 1661, engraving, Florence, Gabinetto Disegni e Stampe degli Uffizi.*

THE 18TH CENTURY

With the death of Gian Gastone de' Medici in 1737, the Medici dynasty came to a close and the Grand Duchy passed to the House of the Habsburg-Lorraine, who governed through a regent until 1765. Although the gardens fell into disuse during these years, a number of radical alterations were undertaken under the direction of Ignazio Pellegrini, such as the construction of a carriageable path linking Bacchus Square to the Amphitheatre and a large chapel that was, however, never completed. Instead, under the Grand Duke Leopoldo de Lorraine (1765 to 1790), numerous modifications were performed on the gardens' sculptural, architectural and water works, as well as on its stone structures and vegetation. New buildings, designed to harmonise with the age-old landscape were also added, amongst which, the Kaffeehaus (1775) and Lemon House (1777-78), both designed by Zanobi del Rosso, and the Meridian Building, begun in 1776 by Niccolò Gaspero Paoletti. Outstanding works of classical sculpture were brought from the

Zanobi del Rosso, The Lemon House, 1777-78.

Villa Medici in Rome, such as the two *Daci Prisoners*, numerous torsos and the Egyptian obelisk, placed in the Amphitheatre's centre in 1790. Further contributions by Pietro Leopoldo were the remodelling of the Meadow of Columns, the creation of a botanical garden near the Specola (currently the Lower Botanical Garden) and the *jardin potager*, intended for the cultivation of exotic vegetables, fruits and flowers (the Upper Botanical Garden).

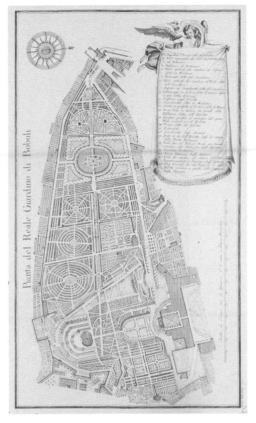

Map of the Gardens from Francesco Maria Soldini's Descrizione, *1790.*

Aniello Lamberti, View of the garden about the Kaffeehaus, ca 1790.

13

THE 19TH AND 20TH CENTURIES

During Napoleon's reign (1799-1814) the gardens once again underwent a period of decline. The intention of the Grand Duchess, Elisa Baciocchi, was to turn Boboli into an English-style garden, a plan never realised for lack of funds. Instead, as the traditional techniques of pruning were abandoned, the es-

View of Boboli Gardens from Pitti Palace in a period image.

paliers and copses consequently grew wild with overgrowth.

The restorative works ordered by the Lorraines once again reestablished the rigorously formal setting that the gardens had had since their origins. The most significant works of this period were the entranceway dubbed 'Annalena', executed after the design of architect Giuseppe Cacialli between 1815 and 1820, the gateway to the Lemon House (1818), and the large Tepidarium of the *jardin potager* (1816), also designed by Cacialli.

In 1834, under Grand Duke Leopoldo II, the gardens suffered the most traumatic remodelling of its long history: the destruction of the labyrinths to make way for a wide carriageable lane, a project undertaken by Pasquale Poccianti, and the diversion of many of the straight paths of the *ragnaie* into curving lanes, after the fashion of the time.

Sometime between 1841 and 1850 the *jardin potager* was transformed into a botanical garden by Filippo Parlatore. Since then Boboli has remained largely unchanged, except for several restorations and the rather sporadic addition of new tree species.

The open-air shows held in the gardens during the current century have enjoyed world renown. It is enough to recall *A Midsummer Night's Dream*, directed by Max Reinhart (1933), Jacques Copeau's rendition of *As You Like It* (1938), *The Tempest*, directed by Giorgio Strehler (1948), Luchino Visconti's *Troilus and Cresida*, (1949) and *The Fairy Queen*, directed by Luca Ronconi (1987).

Filippo Parlatore, Acquarium of the Upper Botanical Garden, latter half of the 19th C.

Due to their very nature, these historical gardens require constant restoration and maintenance. A schedule has therefore been established which provides for their seasonal, yearly and long-term care through periodic renovation and upkeep. Clearly, the architectural components and plant-life are involved more frequently than the inorganic structures of the garden and its decorations, and although the different types of work are not necessarily interdependent, they have been planned for during the same period of time. Moreover, the need to safeguard sculptural works from degradation by atmospheric agents and vandalism often requires housing the originals indoors and replacing them with copies for display. Thus, the gardens' furnishings are necessarily in an incomplete and constantly changing state.

A. AMPHITHEATRE (Anfiteatro)

Interior of the Grotto of Moses.

View of the Artichoke Fountain and Camellia Garden.

Once inside the main entrance of Pitti Palace, one passes through the wide Ammannati courtyard, closed off on three sides by the inner façades of the building and on the fourth by a single storey topped by the Artichoke Fountain (Fontana del Carciofo, 1639-41), the work of Francesco Susini. The middle archway on this side leads to the 17th C Grotto, in whose centre rises the colossal porphyry statue of *Moses*, its base immersed in an elliptical basin.

The entrance to the gardens is to the Grotto's right. The magnificent sight of the Amphitheatre is the first to greet the arriving visitor at the end of the entrance ramp. The masonry foundation was built between 1630 and 1634, after a design by architect Giulio Parigi, and inaugurated in 1637 on the occasion of the coronation of the Grand Duchess of Tuscany, Vittoria della Rovere, wife of Ferdinando II, with the 'Carosello', a choreographic succession inspired by *Gerusalemme Liberata*.

*Giulio Parigi,
Amphitheatre,
completed in 1634.*

*View of the
Amphitheatre from
Pitti Palace with
Roman basin and
Egyptian Obelisk in the
foreground.*

The large arena is surrounded by the six-tiered stands and a balustrade interrupted by twenty-four aedicules which originally held statues, mostly classical, while those on the lateral foundations were of dogs and other animals.

The present arrangement, in which statues alternate with terracotta urns painted to resemble marble, dates back to the work of Giuseppe Cacialli in 1818. In place of the stands, the original Amphitheatre had terraces of beech, oak, ash, olive, fir, cypress and plane-trees.

The cavea, which had been buried during the Lorraine period to construct the carriageable path linking the Bacchus entranceway with Meridian Square, was transformed into a garden decorated with box hedges and potted citrus.

In the Amphitheatre's centre stands the Egyptian Obelisk, brought from the Villa Medici in Rome and set in its current position in 1790, as planned by Niccolò Gaspero Paoletti. The large ancient granite basin also found here was placed in 1840, after the design of Pasquale Poccianti.

B. Forcone Basin (Vasca del Forcone)

Leaving the Amphitheatre behind, we continue along the first landing of the ramp to find two Roman statues, an *Emperor* and a togaed citizen, and in the centre, *Ceres*, a Roman copy of the original Greek statue. Further up we come to the Forcone Basin. This large mixtilinear basin is the result of the modifications carried out by Zanobi del Rosso (1777-78) on the original, rectangular one that acted as a collecting basin for the irrigation waters transported via the aqueduct of Arcetri to the entire area of the gardens. At the centre of the basin stands the bronze statue of *Neptune*, by Soldo Lorenzi, which depicts him brandishing his trident over a cliff on which four marin demi-gods are crouching. The sculptural composition, executed in 1571 for a flower garden once situated to the north of the Palace, was set in its current location in about 1635. The terracing of the surrounding semicircle was originally executed in the 17th century; their present form is the result of 18th century modifications.

Continuing our ascent, to the left we can ad-

Stoldo Lorenzi, Fountain of Neptune with naiads and tritons, bronze and white marble, 1565-68.

mire the spectacle of Fort Belvedere with its imposing walls and behind, Pitti Palace with Florence as its backdrop. Finally, we come to the colossal statue of *Plenty* (*Abbondanza*), begun by Giambologna in 1608 and completed by Pietro Tacca and Sebastiano Salvini (1636-37). At first, conceived of as a portrait of Giovanna of Austria, wife of Francesco I, which would crown a column in Piazza San Marco, it was moved to Boboli in 1636 to represent the prosperity of the Tuscan State, as symbolised by the golden ears of wheat in her left hand and the Cornucopia in her right.

Amongst the trees on the terraces, of particular interest are the plane-trees (*Platanus acerifolia*) planted in the Napoleonic era and pruned to form candelabra.

View of the Fountain of Neptune with Fort Belvedere in the background and the Kaffeehaus on the left.

Giambologna, Piero Tacca, Sebastiano Salvini da Settignano, Plenty, white marble with bronze ears of wheat, 1608, 1636-37.

C. THE KNIGHT'S GARDEN (Giardino del Cavaliere)

The Knight's Garden and Lodge.

Tuscan School, Fountain of the Monkeys, white marble and bronze, 16th-17th C.

Continuing towards the right, we come to the two tenail tiers that lead to the Knight's Garden, offering an enchanting view of the Florentine hills. This garden takes its name from the rampart, known as the 'Bastion of Cavaliere Malatesta' (Malatesta the Knight), which was designed by Michelangelo in 1529. The medicinal plants originally cultivated here, called *semplici*, were replaced by exotic varieties in 1612 when the garden was remodelled after a design by Giulio Parigi. In this same year the Knight's Lodge (*Casino del Cavaliere*) was

built. This is a large room originally utilised to store pots, but subsequently used first by Cardinal Leopoldo de' Medici as a meeting place for scholars and scientists and then in the late 18th C by Cosimo III for the French lessons of his son, Gian Gastone. Today it houses the Porcelain Museum (*Museo delle Porcellane*).

The current arrangement of the garden and its spectacular entranceway date back to the 1792 remodelling by Giuseppe del Rosso, who designed the lower stairway flanked by the two statues of *Muses*, the tenail tiers with circular ramps, as well as the entrance gate overlooked by the marble-painted sandstone *Sphinxes* (by Giovan Battista Giovannozzi, currently in storage) and the garden's box partitions. At the crossroads of the two main paths, we find the Fountain of the Monkeys *(Fontana delle Scimmie):* the marble *putto* are thought to be by either Pierino da Vinci or Stoldo Lorenzi (17th C), while the bronze monkeys are attributable historically to Pietro Tacca (17th C). To the right and left, just under the pillars, are the white marble sculptures of *Jupiter with Eagle* and *Flora*, both attributed to Giovan Battista Caccini (16th C). Lastly, each May the blooming of the 'Banksiae', 'Bourbon' and 'Tea' roses, together with the peonies provides an especially beautiful sight.

Giuseppe del Rosso, entrance to the Knight's Garden, 1792.

Roman copy of original Greek statue of a Muse, *white marble, 2nd C.*

23

D. KAFFEEHAUS

Zanobi del Rosso, the Kaffeehaus, 1774-1775.

Stoldo Lorenzi, Fountain of Ganymede, white marble, 16th-17th C.

Walking out of the Knight's Garden and along the tree-lined path at the foot of Fort Belvedere, we come to the Kaffeehaus. This singular building, designed as a resting place for the Court during their walks through Boboli, was constructed at the wish of Pietro Leopoldo between 1774 and 1775 after the design of Zanobi del Rosso in an airy rococo style. Its original colouring was white and green. The decorations within are by the painters Giuseppe del Moro, Giuliano Traballesi and Pasquale Micheli. On the lawn opposite the Kaffeehaus stands the Fountain of Ganymede; the current figure of Ganymede is a cast of the original marble sculpture executed by Stoldo Lorenzi in the latter half of the 16th C.

E. CYPRESS LANE (Il Viottolone)

From the Kaffeehaus we take a path which, passing Forcone Basin, leads to the beginning of Cypress Lane. This large path (i.e. *Viot-tolone*) makes up the symmetry axis of the expanded gardens, as ordered by Cosimo II and carried out by Giulio Parigi. Planting of the cypresses began in 1612, at the same time as the addition of the labyrinths that used to follow them on the southern side (to the

Roman copy of original Greek statue of Aristogiton, *white marble, 5th C.*

Roman copy of original Greek statue of Harmodius, *white marble, 5th C (cast).*

25

View of the Cerchiata Grande.

left as one descends). Most of these latters were destroyed in 1834, only the three central sections remaining. The entrance onto the lane is flanked by *Aristogiton* on the right and *Harmodius* (cast) on the left, two Roman sculptures copied from Greek originals and restored by Domenico and Giovan Battista Pieratti in 1635. The beginning of the *Viottolone* is still marked by the two citrus groves first planted from 1612 to 1614 according to the traditional arrangement of espaliers of bitter oranges, bordered by a rare red, white and green mosaic marble pavement. The lane is flanked by numerous sculptures, some clas-

Roman copy of original Greek statue of Mercury with Child Bacchus *by Polycletus, (cast).*

Giovan Battista Caccini, Hygieia, *ca 1608 (cast).*

Giovan Battista Caccini, Aesculapius and Hyppolytus, *ca 1608 (cast).*

sical, such as *Mercury with Child Bacchus* (Roman copy of original by Polycletus, replaced by cast), *Young Nero* (Roman art), others from the late 16th C, such as *Hygieia* and *Aesculapius* and *Hyppolytus,* both by Giovanni Caccini and reproduced as copies (ca 1608). The exceptional sculptural group, *Autumn* and *Winter* by Pietro Francavilla (late 16th C) serves to highlight one of the loveliest spots in Boboli, the cross-roads of the *Viottolone* and La Cerchiata ('Latticework'), where a long line of holm-oaks have been pruned to form a continuous 'tunnel'. This was cultivated between 1612 and 1614 together with the two minor latticeworks running alongside the *Viottolone*. From the northern tract, one can reach the Upper Botanical Garden (open only in summer months), created from about 1841 to 1850 by Filippo Parlatore in place of the *jardin potager*, where the visitor can admire the two aquatic-plant pools.

View of the Upper Botanical Garden.

Pietro Francavilla, Autumn *and* Summer, *white marble, late 16th C.*

F. RAGNAIE AND FOUNTAIN OF THE MOSTACCINI

Romolo Ferrucci del Tadda, Fountain of the Mostaccini, pietra forte, 1619-21.

Giambologna, Jupiter white marble on sandstone base, ca 1560.

Walking left along the *Cerchiata*, we then continue down the path formed by the 14th C wall and high espalier of holm-oak and evergreen hedge that is all that remains of the large *Ragnaia della Pace*, designed for bird-hunting with nets. One of the main features of the *ragnaie* were the drinking troughs for birds, a well-preserved example of which is the Fountain of the Mostaccini, formed by a long cascading chain of water gushing from sixteen large, monstrous masks (called *Mostaccini*, perhaps in reference to the moustaches) and terminating below in another water chain devoid of any decoration. The fountain was most likely built between 1619 and 1621 by Romolo Ferrucci del Tadda, author of other animal sculptures found in the gardens. To the left stands the large bust of *Jupiter* (ca 1560) by Giambologna, marking the start of another, typically straight path of the *ragnaie*.

View of the Island Pond.

View of the Island Pond with the Harpies and Ocean Fountains in the foreground and Cypress Lane behind.

Orazio Mochi, Romolo Ferrucci del Tadda, Gioco del saccomazzone, *pietra serena, before 1621.*

Giovan Battista *Capezzuoli,* Gioco della pentolaccia, *white marble, 1780.*

G. ISLAND POND (Vasca dell'Isola)
(Accessible only in May and June)

Towards the end of the *Viottolone* to the left one can see the sculptural group, the *Saccomazzone* by Orazio Mochi and Romolo Ferrucci del Tadda (17th C), while Giovan Battista Capezzuoli's *Gioco della Pentolaccia* ('the clay-pot game') (18th C) stands on the right. We thus come to the Island Square *(Piaz-zale dell'Isola).* The pond itself is made up of a large oval basin with the small island in its centre. The island can be reached by two paths running parallel to the *Viottolone.* The open space of the square is bordered by a tall espalier of hedge and holm-oak with numerous niches holding 17th C statues, mostly from the Florentine school and nearly all depicting peasants or hunters, according to an aesthetic sense for themes befitting the gardens' bucolic atmosphere.

Noteworthy examples are the *Moor Hunter* by Giovan Battista Pieratti, the *Hunter with Sparrow-hawk* by Domenico Pieratti, and

Period photo of the Island Pond entrance gate with columns topped by capricorns.

Tuscan School, Peasant, *pietra serena, 17th C.*

Domenico Pieratti, Wrestler, *pietra serena, 1654.*

Giovan Simone Cioli, Youth, *pietra serena, 1599-1608.*

the *Youth* by Giovan Simone Cioli. The pond's borders were originally equipped with a continuous series of water jets. Now, on its northern and southernmost points, we find the two Fountains of Loves executed respectively by Giovan Battista and Domenico Pieratti, and Cosimo Salvestrini and Giovan Francesco Su-sini between 1623 and 1624, and at the eastern and western ends, the Harpies Fountains, late 18th C copies by Innocenzo Spinazzi of the 17th C originals, probably designed by Giulio Parigi.

Access to the Island is through two gates upheld by paired sandstone columns topped by the marble *Capri-corns* symbolising Cosimo I de' Medici that were partly restored or redone in the 18th C by Giovan Battista Capezzuoli. Immersed in the pond's waters we can see *Perseus*, restored by Giovan Battista Pieratti, and *Andromeda*, attributed to this same artist. In the island's centre we find Giambologna's 1576 Ocean

Perseus on horseback,
*white marble, 1636-37,
restored by Giovan
Battista Pieratti.*

*Giovan Battista
Pieratti*, Andromeda,
white marble, 1636-37.

Fountain (*Fontana dell'Oceano*), originally located in the Amphitheatre's arena and moved here in 1636. The colossal *Ocean*, an early 20th C copy by Raffaello Romanelli of the original now held in the Museo del Bargello, rises above the pedestal, about which are arranged the Nile, Ganges and Euphrates rivers. The pedestal is adorned with sculpted bas-reliefs depicting mythological scenes: the *Rape of Europa*, *Diana Bathing* and the *Triumph of Neptune*. The fountain's basin is made from a single granite block, transported from the Island of Elba by order of Cosimo I and sculpted by Il Tribolo in 1550. The surrounding garden, with nearly two hun-dred potted citrus trees, maintains the original design, while an ancient rose collection has recently been reconstructed within the flower-beds. The surrounding flower-beds are adorned with 17th and 18th C varieties of bulbous plants.

Giovan Francesco Susini and Giovan Battista Pieratti, Putto shooting an arrow *and* Putto breaking a heart with a hammer, *white marble, 1624.*

Giambologna, The Ocean Fountain, white marble and Elba granite, 1576.

H. MEADOW OF COLUMNS (Prato delle Colonne)

Continuing onto the wide semicircle which links the Island Pond with the area of the Roman Gate (*Porta Romana*), we come to the Meadow of Columns. The gravel path parallel to the *Viottolone* divides the meadow into two sectors, in the centre of which stand the two red porphyry columns, of uncertain origins, placed here between 1775 and 1779. Their layout is by Gaspero Niccolò Paoletti, who also executed the bases and crowns, made up of capitals topped by marble urns. Along the hedges ringing the meadow are twelve colossal busts, some original Roman sculptures, others, Roman copies of Greek originals, and still others, classical elements contaminated by late-Renaissance insertions.

Among the most noteworthy are the *Bearded Hero* from the Villa Medici in Rome, and so-called *Trajan* and *Pyrrhus*. The Meadow once held *Aesculapius*, from the Villa in Pratolino, attributed to Stoldo Lorenzi, and *Saturn*, by Gherardo Silvani (1621), both currently in storage. Along the small path leading to the Roman Gates we find the singular sculptural

View of the Meadow of Columns.

Roman copy of original Greek statue of Pyrrhus, *white marble, 2nd C (the head is a 16th C addition).*

Roman Art, the so-called Trajan, *white marble, 2nd C (?).*

34

group of grotesque figures called the *Caramogi*, by Romolo Ferrucci del Tadda (1619-20), while opposite these is the *Owl Game* (1780), by Giovan Battista Capezzuoli, based on the original work of Romolo Ferrucci del Tadda. Near the Roman Gate stands Vincenzo Danti's *Perseus* (1577), and at its base, the beautiful Roman sarcophagus depicting the *Trials of Hercules*, by Lisippus (2nd C).

Above:
Romolo Ferrucci del Tadda, Three grotesque figures, *pietra serena, 1617-21.*

Roman Art, copy by Giovan Battista Capezzuoli of Romolo Ferrucci del Tadda's original, The Owl Game, *white marble, 1617-21.*

Below*:*
Vincenzo Danti, Perseus and the monster, *white marble, 1573-85.*

Roman Art, copy of original by Lisippus, sarcophagus with the Trials of Hercules, *white marble, 2nd C.*

at left:
Tuscan School, (Stoldo Lorenzi?), Aesculapius, *white marble, latter half of 16th C.*

35

I. ANNALENA GROTTO

Michelangelo Naccherini, Adam and Eve, *detail with the mosaic vault of the Annalena Grotto in the background.*

opposite page:
Valerio and Giovan Simone Cioli, Harvest Fountain, *white marble, 1599-1608.*

Valerio and Giovan Simone Cioli, Peasant with spade, *white marble, 1599-1608.*

via Romana.

The interior decoration with sponges and large masks shows evident traces of Bernardo Buontalenti's marvellous innovations in the Grand Grotto, however with a measured distancing from this latter evincing Cacialli's personal reflections on Renaissance decorative models and their reinterpretation in a contemporary manner.

The ceiling, made up of bright sea-blue panels with yellowish orange bordering, depicts the attributes of the god of the seas, Poseidon, with his entourage: tridents, shells and corals, surrounded by minute concretions simulating the stalactites of a natural grotto and abundant *Haliotis lamellosa*, the shells of a very common species rich in mother of pearl. A recent restoration has brought out the vivacious tones of the ceiling and the warm hue of the Pratolino sponges which, suspended from the ceiling, provide a pleasant contrast to the white marble of the large masks, created in the same period by Ottaviano Giovanozzi after the design of the grotto's architect, Giuseppe Cacialli.

In 1817 the architect Giuseppe Cacialli created the small Annalena Grotto beside the entranceway in via Romana. The fine sculptural group of *Adam and Eve* (1616?) by Michelangelo Naccherino (1550-1622) was taken from one of the hanging gardens at the top of the *Viottolone* and placed in the grotto.

The neo-classical architecture of the Grotto is reminiscent of the series of modifications carried out by Cacialli between 1815 and 1820 in order to enhance and enlarge the entrance in

J. LEMON HOUSE (Limonaia)

Flanking the garden's borders along the Lemon House path are the *Peasant with spade* and Harvest Fountain, both by Valerio and Giovan Simone Cioli (1599-1608).

Just down the path we come to the Lemon House, built from 1777 to 1778 after the design of Zanobi del Rosso as a substitute for the former Menagerie and its collection of rare animals which was dismantled by order of Grand Duke Pietro Leopoldo de Lorraine. The rococo façade pre-

serves its original colours, and the building is still used today to store the collection of nearly five hundred potted citrus plants, one of the most typical characteristics of Tuscan gardens. The Medici held citrus trees in high esteem, both for their therapeutic and aromatic value, as well as for their unique beauty. Still today many rare and unique varieties are cultivated here. The box flower-bed opposite the Lemon House reflects the original 18th C design, and is now used to cultivate ancient varieties of roses, camellia and bulb plants. The wall is topped by classical statues depicting the *Muses*, a *Bagpiper* and *Dwarf.* Also worthy of note is the beautiful wrought-iron gate designed by Giuseppe Cacialli in 1817.

Roman Art, pair of Muses, *white marble, 2nd C.*

Tuscan School, The Bagpiper, *white marble, 17th C.*

K. MERIDIAN BUILDING (Palazzina della Meridiana)

Nicolò Gaspero Paoletti and Pasquale Poccianti, Meridian Building, 1766-1832.

View of the hill opposite the Meridian Building.

Continuing along the Lemon House path to Pitti Palace, on the left we find the Meridian Building, at present housing the Costume Museum (Museo del Costume), which Pietro Leopoldo de Lorraine had built to equip the royal residence with more practical apartments than the uncomfortable quarters in Pitti Palace. It was begun around 1776 by Niccolò Gaspero Paoletti and completed in 1832 by architect Pasquale Poccianti. The ramps leading to the Chestnut grove and *Viottolone* were also added by Paoletti to the sloping grounds in front of the building, once used as a stone quarry. In the centre of the first ramp stands the winged horse, called *Pegasus* (late 16th C), restored by Aristodemo Costoli in 1865. Looking out the parapet towards Palazzo Pitti, one can view the Camellia Garden, an 19th C camellia collection in a garden created during the 17th C.

View of the Meridian Hill showing a Roman-art basin and in the background, Pegasus, *by unknown late 16th C artist restored by Artistodemo Costoli in 1865.*

Roman Art, Statues of the Emperors Augustus *and* Marcus Aurelius *in lorica, white marble, 2nd C.*

Walking past Pitti Palace towards the exit, we come to the wide Bacchus Square, which gets its name from the singular statue situated near the exit gate. Though known to the Florentines as 'Bacchus', the statue is actually the *Dwarf Morgante*, depicted by Valerio Cioli astride a turtle (currently replaced by a copy). Entering the wide carriageable path, we find the *Daci Prisoners*, porphyry Roman statues from the Villa Medici collection in Rome, and dating back to the 2nd C (the white marble heads were likely added in the 16th C). The two white marble bases are also worthy of note: sculpted with trophies, barbarians, Dioskouroi and Victories, likely taken from a Roman triumphal arch from the 3rd C.

L. BACCHUS SQUARE
(Piazzale di Bacco)

Valerio Cioli, Dwarf Morgante, *white marble, 1560.*

Roman Art, Daci Prisoners, *porphyry and white marble, 2nd C.*

M. Buontalenti's Grotto (Grand Grotto)
Grotta del Buontalenti (Grotta Grande)

(Visits permitted only upon authorisation)

View of the first chamber's interior.

Along the boundary of the gardens, on the northern side of Bacchus Square, we come to this grotto, also known as the Grand Grotto. Its current appearance is the result of modification of the original plant nursery built by Giorgio Vasari between 1557 and 1560 in the last section of the corridor linking Palazzo Vecchio and Pitti Palace, which was also designed by Vasari together with the façade and loggia of the entrance with its columns

Giorgio Varsari and Bernardo Buontalenti, façade of the Grand Grotto, detail and outside view, 1557-60.

in red Monterantoli stone and while marble bases and capitals. Between 1583 and 1587 the nursery was transformed into a grotto according to the design of Bernardo Buontalenti.

In 1587 Giovanni Battista del Tadda decorated the façade with the 'rustic' figures, *Peace* and *Justice* (or *Harmony*?), as well as the emblems of Cosimo I and a *Capricorn* and *Turtle*.

In the niches flanking the entrance are Baccio Bandinelli's statues of *Bacchus* and *Ceres* (1552-56). The interior walls of the first room were decorated by Pietro Mati in a spongy material with a bas-relief series inspired by the myth of Deucalion and Pyrrha. In 1585 Buontalenti placed Michelangelo's *Prisoners* in the grotto's corners (the originals, now housed in the Museo dell'Accademia, were replaced with white con-

crete castes in 1924). The ceiling and wall frescoes by the ruins of a cupola were painted by Bernardino Poccetti (1886-87) and depict various animal species. It is said that the circular opening in the vault was once filled by a hollow crystal ball with fish swimming in. Water once gushed forth from encrustations throughout the walls, creating spectacular effects as the wet mate-rials glistened in all their chromatic glory. In 1587 the sculptural group, *Theseus and Helen*, by Vincenzo de' Rossi was placed in the second chamber, while in 1593 Giambologna's masterpiece *Venus* was set in the centre of the third, most secretive room on a green African marble bowl upheld by white marble satyrs. The wall frescoes by Bernardino Poccetti portray an arbour with birds flying about its vines. Giovan Battista del Tadda (1589) created the mountain-shaped fountains in the corner niches, while the terracotta anthropomorphic masks in the vault's cornice are by Gualtieri di Jacopo Gonnelli (1585-86).

Bernardino Poccetti, ceiling frescoes of the Grand Grotto.

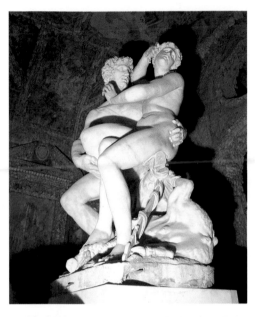

Vincenzo de' Rossi,
Theseus and Helen,
1587.

*View of the third
chamber's vault.*

Giambologna, Venus,
1593.

N. Grotto of Madam (Grotticina di Madama)

Davide Fortini, Grotto of Madam, sculpture by Baccio Bandinelli and Giovan Paolo Fancelli, white marble and pietra serena, 1553-55.

Leaving Buontalenti's Grotto towards the left, we encounter the Grotto of Madam, Boboli's oldest.

It was commissioned by Eleonora of Toledo and carried out between 1553 and 1555 under the direction of Davide Fortini. The interior is decorated with a spongy material and stalactites. The sculptures are by Baccio Bandinelli and Giovanni di Paolo Fancelli. The vault frescoes have been attributed to Francesco Ubertini, known as 'Il Bachiacca' (1554-55), while the splendid two-coloured terracotta floor is the work of Santi Buglioni.

Boboli is the consummate garden *alla italiana*. Its paths are lined by high hedges composed of holm-oaks (*Quercus ilex*) in their upper portions and various shrub species below (*Viburnum tinus, Laurus nobilis, Phillyrea latifolia, Rhamnus alaternus, Myrtus communis*). The inner copses are also made up mostly of holm-oaks, though a number of deciduous plants are also represented: the plane trees (*Platanus acerifolia*) of the Forcone and the Meadow of Columns, as well as a *Ginkgo biloba*, an *Acer monspessulanum* and two *Liriodendron tulipifera*. The cedars include, amongst the predominant Atlantic and deodar species, a single specimen of *Cedrus libani* in the Lower Botanical Garden.

The potted citrus collection is amongst the largest in Europe, and the roses in the gardens of the Island's Lemon House include many exquisite varieties, such as 'Chapeau de Napoléon', 'Madame Pierre Ogier', 'Complicata', 'Tuscany Superb', 'Variegata di Bologna', 'Ferdinand Pichard' and 'Cardinal de Richelieu'. The Upper Botanical Garden also holds an interesting collection of aquatic plants, including *Euryale ferox, Glyceria acquatica, Victoria regia, Hybiscus militaris, Dion spinolosum* and *Pandanus utilis*.

Camellia Garden, late 17th C.

Garden of the Lemon House, autumn blossoms.

Garden of the Island, citrus trees and roses.

The Ragnaia della stella.

Decoration of the Annalena Grotto vault.

printed in October 1998
by Media Print-Livorno
for
s i l l a b e